CHARLIE WAITE'S
SPANISH LANDSCAPES

North of Fiscal, province of Huesca

CHARLIE WAITE'S
SPANISH
LANDSCAPES

TEXT BY THE DUKE OF WELLINGTON

HAMISH HAMILTON · LONDON

HAMISH HAMILTON LTD

Published by the Penguin Group
Penguin Books Ltd, 27 Wrights Lane, London W8 5TZ, England
Penguin Books USA Inc., 375 Hudson Street, New York, New York 10014, USA
Penguin Books Australia Ltd, Ringwood, Victoria, Australia
Penguin Books Canada Ltd, 10 Alcorn Avenue, Toronto, Ontario, Canada M4V 3B2
Penguin Books (NZ) Ltd, 182–190 Wairau Road, Auckland 10, New Zealand

Penguin Books Ltd, Registered Offices: Harmondsworth, Middlesex, England

First published 1992
1 3 5 7 9 10 8 6 4 2

Printed in Singapore by Toppan Printing Co., Ltd

A CIP catalogue record for this book is available from the British Library

ISBN 0–241–12807–2

THE PHOTOGRAPHS IN THIS BOOK
ARE FOR MY DEAR SISTER JOANNA

EAST OF JACA, PROVINCE OF HUESCA

LIST OF PHOTOGRAPHS

EAST OF BENALUP DE SIDONIA, PROVINCE OF CÁDIZ

INTRODUCTION

There used to be a cliché much quoted in guide books that 'Spain is different'. Certainly many aspects of Spanish life still set her apart from other countries of Western Europe, and no aspect is more different and distinctive than the countryside of the Iberian peninsula. A traveller with resolution and stamina could, if he so wished, pass through in a few days landscapes as different from each other as the wooded valleys of Wales and the fringes of the Sahara Desert. He could see gorges lined with fantastic rock formations, vast escarpments and cliffs pock-marked with caves (many of which were inhabited until quite recently by troglodytes), heather moorlands, huge plains with limitless horizons, snow-capped mountains to rival the Alps, endless stretches of rocky, arid country, palm-fringed shorelines, paddy-fields and fields of sugar cane, olive groves and vineyards, orchards of oranges and avocados, cork forests and huge areas of scrub-covered hill given over to cattle or a fantastic variety of wildlife. Our intrepid traveller would also be astonished at the scale of the landscapes he passed through. Spain is a very 'big' country in Western European terms.

How has this enormous variety of landscapes come about? Above all, the forces of nature and climate are responsible, but there is another force – that of isolation from outside influences. Spain is bounded by high mountains in the north and by the Bay of Biscay, the Atlantic and the Mediterranean on the other sides. This natural isolation has been compounded for long periods by an inward preoccupation enforced by man. In prehistoric times and later, Spain drew men from many parts of Europe in search of land and minerals, such as copper and iron. Phoenicians, Romans, Jews and Visigoths amongst others came, liked what they found and stayed, but in AD 711 an invasion of a new sort occurred. In that year the first wave of Muslim invaders landed on the shores of southern Spain and in a few years had engulfed the whole country.

Much of Spain remained under Muslim domination for several centuries and some parts of the south for as long as eight centuries – almost equivalent to the time-span in England between today and Norman times. Muslim domination had a most profound effect on Spain. In other parts of Europe great forces of change were on the move, but Spain remained largely isolated from these. The Moors, however, were remarkably tolerant. Christians and Jews were allowed to follow their religions and cultures. The arts and sciences flourished and universities sprang up. Córdoba became one of the most important cultural centres in Europe in spite of being largely cut off from outside influences. In agriculture the Moors had a lasting effect on the countryside, beneficial in some areas, less so in others. It is said that in prehistoric times a squirrel could have travelled from the Pyrenees to the Straits of Gibraltar without touching ground. Although they were masters of the art of irrigation and made full use of Spanish water resources, the Moors also cleared large areas of forest for cultivation and the production of charcoal. The goats and sheep which followed these changes inhibited natural forest regeneration and the inevitable erosion occurred. Many of the stony wastes, deserts and extraordinary rock formations that we see in Spain today result from the erosion that started in this period and continued throughout the centuries. Yet in those parts of the country where water was available, the Moors' skills have left a valuable legacy. Even today, in the area around Granada where they established thriving farms for crops and vegetables, the original channels to bring water from the Sierra Nevada are used for gardens, fountains and the production of fruit.

In the north the militant Christianity which

spawned the Crusades began to drive the 'Muslim Infidel' back towards Africa. Gradually the Moorish dominance declined and their forces fell back towards the south. In their wake the Christian princelings and Catholic potentates vied for power and influence. They established their fiefdoms and built their castles and religious houses to re-establish the Christian faith and maintain their power and influence. Today, many of those castles stand as gaunt ruins dominating an empty countryside, but they remind us, if we take a second look, that once they commanded an important route or river crossing. Life in the countryside in those days was often violent and dangerous. Warring factions and the banditry which plagued Spain for many centuries forced men to group together for mutual protection in tightly packed villages, often in some high place or in the lee of the castle of a ruling nobleman. Men would daily leave their sanctuaries and walk miles to work their land because it simply wasn't safe to live in the countryside. As a result, even now and especially in the Meseta, the high plateau interspersed with mountains or sierrras which cover the whole of central Spain, there are vast areas with barely a house on them. Many of the villages remain much as they were in the Middle Ages but are increasingly deserted by the young people, who leave to seek employment in the industrial areas. The Meseta has always been a harsh environment to work in. Much of the soil is poor and

stony. In summer it is hot and dusty, and in winter can be extremely cold with its bare, windswept landscapes. But in spring and early summer it suddenly discards its brown and grey mantle and almost overnight becomes a place of enchantment with its mixture of greens and patches of wild flowers including, of course, great swathes of scarlet poppies.

When the Christian reconquest was completed with the fall of the last Moorish kingdom of Granada in 1492, Spain could boast at last of being a united realm under Ferdinand and Isabella. The following two centuries saw a tremendous thrust of Spanish expansion overseas. The year 1492 also saw the discovery of America by Christopher Columbus, and during the sixteenth and seventeenth centuries the Conquistadores, many of whom came from Extremadura, the poorest province of Spain, poured the great wealth they had acquired in the Americas back into the cities of their province such as Cáceres and Trujillo and into the coffers of Spain. They built great palaces in the towns, but the countryside remained poor, neglected and bandit-ridden. One exception was the great marsh extending westwards from Granada, where the Habsburg kings settled men from all over Spain, many of them convicts, to turn this huge area of malarial marsh into one of the most fertile and productive areas of all Spain.

The eighteenth and early nineteenth centuries saw Spain after the War of the Spanish Succession experiencing a period of retrenchment and comparative peace. The one exception was the five traumatic years of what we call the Peninsular War and the Spaniards La Guerra de Independencia. British soldiers in their diaries and letters speak of the hardships they suffered in that campaign as they marched endlessly across dusty plains on appalling roads or, even worse, through the mud of those same roads after rain. From their descriptions it is clear that the landscapes haven't changed much in almost two hundred years. Perhaps there are fewer trees because of the insatiable demand, until quite recently, for charcoal. As recently as thirty years ago most of the side roads in Spain were still made of dirt – dusty in summer and muddy and rutted in winter.

Much of the nineteenth century was characterized by the instability created by the Carlist wars. Banditry still flourished and made life in the country hazardous; so much so that even the nobles deserted their castles and migrated to grand houses in the larger cities. By so doing, they further contributed to the neglect of the countryside. A hundred and thirty years ago an ancestor of mine decided to visit the family property near Granada. Communications over land were still so bad that he decided to sail to Málaga and then proceed by carriage, with a mule train for the baggage, through the mountains to Granada. He was eventually dissuaded from undertaking this hazardous journey because of the fear of bandits, in spite of being promised an escort of cavalry. Bandit chiefs literally ruled over large areas of the more remote countryside until law and order were eventually established by the setting up of the Guardia Civil in the rural areas. Even so there was an upsurge of this banditry after the Civil War in the forties and fifties. Such lawlessness led to a reluctance to travel freely in the countryside, but the result is that today we can see unspoilt and deserted landscapes much as they were hundreds of years ago. Bandits and banditry are part of the folklore of Spain and for that we must take some pleasure. I did not take so benign a view when in 1951 my wife and I were strongly advised to get through the Sierra Morena, the mountains to the north of Granada, before nightfall because of the fear of bandits! However, we arrived at our destination without incident, the only serious hazard being a near miss on a corner after dark with a bullock cart lit only by a dim hurricane lamp slung from the axle between the rear wheels.

That journey, over forty years ago, lives on in my memory as it was the first time my wife and I visited our family property near Granada given to my ancestor, the 1st Duke, in 1811 by the Cortes of Spain in gratitude for his victory over the French at Salamanca. We drove for eleven hours from Madrid in an ancient pre-war Citroën on a narrow and, in places, winding piece of tarmac bounded on both sides by a wide donkey track. There was little traffic except for a steady stream of donkeys and mule- and bullock-carts on the tracks beside the road. For hour after hour we drove over the vast stretches of the Mancha with its limitless horizons and distant views of mountain ranges. It was early winter and much of the earth was red-brown with an occasional patch of winter corn showing pale green in the wintry sunshine. Apart from the occasional village the landscape was bereft of all buildings except the odd distant silhouette of a ruin against the horizon. Should we go and look at it? No – must get on and through the dreaded Sierra Morena!

As we neared the south of the Mancha there seemed to be more human activity. Vineyards started to be commonplace, many of them still had their crimson leaves, but pruning was under way and the carts were moving in a steady stream with the unwanted branches towards Valdepeñas and the surrounding villages. Soon we were in the foothills of the Sierra Morena. The road wound through steep mountains and spectacular gorges – perfect bandit country – and with memories of pushing through not dissimilar country in Italy after the retreating Germans only seven years before, those beautiful hillsides took on a more sinister appearance. We passed through the village of La Carolina, said to be the heart of bandit activity, and, in spite of its reputation, found it rather charming. A few hours later we at last arrived, just as it was getting dark, on the edge of the great plain of Granada. It didn't take us long, after surviving the incident with the bullock-cart, to drive under the aqueduct built by Godoy, Chief Minister to Charles IV, to bring water to the olive-oil mill and pass through the stone pillars encrusted with W's which mark the entrance to the Molino del Rey (the Mill of the King), the property which before its grant to my ancestor had been in the ownership of the Kings of Spain for three hundred years and before that the Sultans of Granada. We followed the drive up the hill built by my grandfather because he thought the old drive too steep for his horses, and arrived at the house which, for the first thirty-five years of my life, had been just a name to me. After the welcoming formalities we tumbled into bed after what seemed a very long day.

We awoke to a new and enchanting world. Stretched out below us to the east were row upon row of olive trees standing out dark against the pink earth. Gradually the olives merged into the flat irrigated plain of the Vega of Granada, stretching right up to the edge of the city thirty miles away. In those days the plain was dotted with villages but precious few other buildings except occasional tobacco sheds, beautiful in their own right with their perforated sides and tiled roofs. Dominating the whole plain was the great range of the Sierra Nevada capped with snow and sparkling white in the winter sun. It includes, at 12,000 feet, the second highest peak in Europe, the Mulhacén. Somewhere under the rocks at the summit lie the bones of the last Sultan of Granada, but his grave is known only to Allah. That view for us remains the most spectacular in the world.

In the days that followed we found ourselves in an agricultural world that had changed little since the last century. Stooks of wheat were being threshed on the threshing floors by a mule going round and round and drawing a platform with serrated edges underneath. On the platform sat a man directing the mule. At the end of the process the grain was winnowed by gangs of men with large, flat, wooden shovels and the chaff was stacked. On other parts of the estate herds of mares for producing mules wandered with a herdsman. Elsewhere were black and red pigs scavenging for acorns and grain. Flocks of black fat-tailed sheep for producing astrakhan grazed on the stubble, and mule teams were hard at work ploughing. The picture was to change rapidly in the next few years, but in 1951 Spain was a poor country and still ostracized by many countries in Europe.

Not long ago my wife and I undertook, for the umpteenth time, the drive from Madrid to the Molino del Rey. Now there is a dual carriageway practically the whole way. Motels, bars, souvenir shops, petrol stations and even factories proliferate and the drive takes half the time. Even the Sierra Morena has been planted with trees and has lost its sinister associations. La Carolina has been by-passed but is full of souvenir shops selling ceramics, straw donkeys and the like. The plain of Granada is still very beautiful but sprouts functional onion and potato sheds like mushrooms. There is, alas, often a film of smog hanging over Granada, but the Sierra Nevada still dominates the landscape in all its

beauty. At the Molino del Rey most of the animals have disappeared, but the sheep are still there wandering the hillsides and their bells delight the ear. Some of the olives have gone and in their place are great fields of irrigated crops.

I have tried to trace the evolution of the Spanish countryside and its landscapes. Charlie Waite has captured these to a remarkable degree in this book of his photographs. Here we can see the olives and their shadows, black against the white clay they love to grow in, the great escarpments and the river valleys, the fields of poppies in the Meseta in the spring and a wealth of contrasting scenes of this extraordinary country. It is a wonderful record of a countryside which has changed little in hundreds of years. Of course in the years to come change it will for all sorts of reasons, but at least there will always be this captivating book to show what it once looked like.

His Grace the Duke of Wellington and Ciudad Rodrigo, KG, LVO, OBE, MC, DL

EAST OF GUARDO, PROVINCE OF LEÓN　　　　15

NORTH OF PORZUNA, PROVINCE OF TOLEDO

SOUTH OF OYARZÚN, PROVINCE OF GUIPÚZCOA

NEAR VALENCIA, PROVINCE OF LÉRIDA

NORTH OF PONT DE SUERT, PROVINCE OF LÉRIDA

SENEGÜE, NORTH-WEST OF SABIÑÁNIGO, PROVINCE OF HUESCA

EAST OF ARCOS DE LA FRONTERA, PROVINCE OF CÁDIZ

SIERRA DE LA PANDERA, PROVINCE OF JAÉN

SOUTH OF BIESCAS, PROVINCE OF HUESCA

GUADALEST, PROVINCE OF ALICANTE

EAST OF RONDA, PROVINCE OF MÁLAGA   27

North of Molina de Aragón, province of Guadalajara

SOUTH OF SORT, VALLE DE LLESÚY, PROVINCE OF LÉRIDA   29

NORTH OF PAMPLONA, PROVINCE OF NAVARRA

RIVER SEGRE, NORTH OF ORGAÑA, PROVINCE OF LÉRIDA   31

WEST OF HUELMA, PROVINCE OF JAÉN

SOUTH OF ALGUEÑA, PROVINCE OF ALICANTE   33

EAST OF RONDA, PROVINCE OF MÁLAGA

EAST OF ESCÓ, PROVINCE OF NAVARRA

SIERRA DE MONTSERRAT, PROVINCE OF BARCELONA

SOUTH OF RÍPODAS, PROVINCE OF NAVARRA

MONTE PERDIDO, ORDESA NATIONAL PARK, PROVINCE OF HUESCA

VENTOSA, EAST OF NÁJERA, PROVINCE OF LOGROÑO   39

ARSÉGUEL, PROVINCE OF LÉRIDA

NEAR GUADALEST, PROVINCE OF ALICANTE 41

SOUTH OF PONT DE SUERT, PROVINCE OF LÉRIDA

WEST OF TORDESILLAS, PROVINCE OF VALLADOLID

43

WEST OF GUADALUPE, PROVINCE OF CÁCERES

46   CAPILEIRA, SOUTH OF GRANADA, PROVINCE OF GRANADA

SOUTH OF LA BARBOLLA, PROVINCE OF GUADALAJARA

EAST OF BUJALANCE, PROVINCE OF CÓRDOBA   49

SOUTH OF MESTANZA, PROVINCE OF CIUDAD REAL

ALGATOCÍN, PROVINCE OF MÁLAGA

ALGATOCÍN, PROVINCE OF MÁLAGA

SOUTH OF UBRIQUE, PROVINCE OF CÁDIZ

SOUTH OF LAS CUEVAS, PROVINCE OF ALICANTE   55

SOUTH OF HUELMA, PROVINCE OF JAÉN

SETENIL, PROVINCE OF CADÍZ   57

58   EAST OF CÓRDOBA, PROVINCE OF CÓRDOBA

EAST OF CHELVA, PROVINCE OF VALENCIA

NORTH OF ALMAGRO, PROVINCE OF CIUDAD REAL

SOUTH OF JIMENA DE LA FRONTERA, PROVINCE OF CÁDIZ

NORTH OF MORELLA, PROVINCE OF CASTELLÓN DE LA PLANA

NORTH-WEST OF PONT DE SUERT, COLL DE ESPINA, PROVINCE OF HUESCA

PUENTE DE MONTAÑANA, WEST OF TREMP, PROVINCE OF LÉRIDA 67

NORTH OF GUADIX, PROVINCE OF GRANADA

SIERRA DE LA PANDERA, PROVINCE OF JAÉN

SOUTH OF GRAZALEMA, PROVINCE OF CÁDIZ

SOUTH OF MOLINILLO, PROVINCE OF CIUDAD REAL   71

VALLE DE ANSÓ, PROVINCE OF HUESCA

Gerri de la Sal, Province of Lérida

EAST OF RONDA, PROVINCE OF MÁLAGA

NORTH OF BARÓ, VALLE DE LLESÚY, PROVINCE OF LÉRIDA   75

River Ésera, south of Campo, province of Huesca

SALARDÚ, VALLE DE ARÁN, PROVINCE OF LÉRIDA

EAST OF OLVERA, PROVINCE OF CÁDIZ

NEAR BOLTAÑA, PROVINCE OF HUESCA

SOUTH OF BERLANGA DE DUERO, PROVINCE OF SORIA

EAST OF AINSA, PROVINCE OF HUESCA

ORDESA NATIONAL PARK, PROVINCE OF HUESCA

NORTH OF EL CAMPO, PROVINCE OF CÁCERES

83

RIBADÉO, PROVINCE OF LUGO

WEST OF TORDESILLAS, PROVINCE OF VALLADOLID

SIERRA DE GREDOS, NORTH OF ARENAS, PROVINCE OF ÁVILA

NORTH OF BURGUI, PROVINCE OF NAVARRA

NORTH OF SIGÜENZA, PROVINCE OF GUADALAJARA

EAST OF GÁLVEZ, PROVINCE OF TOLEDO

GAUCÍN, PROVINCE OF MÁLAGA

SOUTH OF MORÓN DE LA FRONTERA, PROVINCE OF SEVILLA

NORTH OF ALMAGRO, PROVINCE OF CIUDAD REAL

94   SOUTH OF VIELLA, PROVINCE OF LÉRIDA

BAGERQUE, VALLE DE ARÁN, PROVINCE OF LÉRIDA

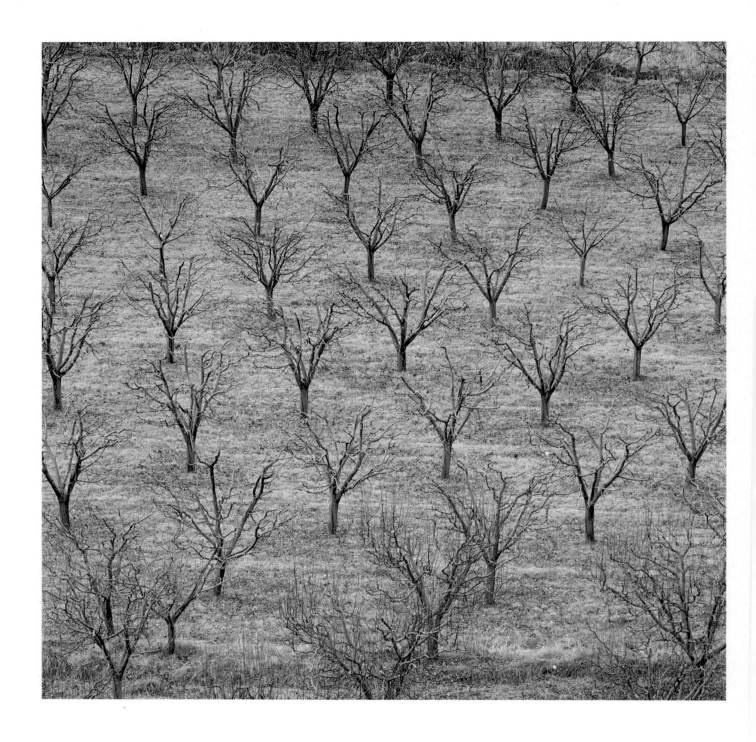

NORTH OF BERDÚN, PROVINCE OF HUESCA

NORTH-EAST OF MASEGOSO, PROVINCE OF GUADALAJARA

SOUTH OF BENASQUE, PROVINCE OF HUESCA

SIERRA DE GREDOS, PROVINCE OF ÁVILA

NORTH OF BENAOJÁN, PROVINCE OF MÁLAGA

NORTH OF VILLARCAYO, PROVINCE OF BURGOS

NORTH-EAST OF SANGÜESA, PROVINCE OF NAVARRA

RIVER JÚCAR, EAST OF CUENCA, PROVINCE OF CUENCA   103

SIERRA DE CHIMENEA, SOUTH OF ANTEQUERA, PROVINCE OF MÁLAGA

WEST OF MALAGÓN, PROVINCE OF CIUDAD REAL

RIVER ESLA, WEST OF ZAMORA, PROVINCE OF ZAMORA

NORTH OF AINSA, PROVINCE OF HUESCA

LACALAHORRA, EAST OF GUADIX, PROVINCE OF GRANADA

CASARES, PROVINCE OF MÁLAGA

CASAS ALTAS, RINCÓN DE ADEMUZ, PROVINCE OF VALENCIA   111

SOUTH OF RIAÑO, PROVINCE OF LEÓN

RIVER ÉSERA, SOUTH OF CAMPO, PROVINCE OF HUESCA

114   EAST OF ILLORA, PROVINCE OF GRANADA

GRAZALEMA, PROVINCE OF CÁDIZ   115

116   EAST OF SEGOVIA, PROVINCE OF SEGOVIA

JARANDILLA DE LA VERA, PROVINCE OF CÁCERES 117

EAST OF RONCAL, PROVINCE OF NAVARRA

NORTH OF PINOS-PUENTE, PROVINCE OF GRANADA

SOUTH OF AOIZ, PROVINCE OF NAVARRA

RIVER EBRO, LA RIOJA

SOUTH OF SOLSONA, PROVINCE OF LÉRIDA

NORTH OF NAVALVILLAR DE IBOR, PROVINCE OF CÁCERES 123

South of Liérganes, province of Santander

TORRE ALHÁQUIME, SOUTH-EAST OF OLVERA, PROVINCE OF CÁDIZ 125

EAST OF CARAVACA DE LA CRUZ, PROVINCE OF MURCIA

NORTH OF BRIONES, PROVINCE OF LOGROÑO

128   West of Malagón, province of Ciudad Real

SOUTH OF ORIHUELA DEL TREMEDAL, PROVINCE OF TERUEL   129

Sierra de Montserrat, province of Barcelona

VANDELLÓS, PROVINCE OF TARRAGONA 131

132   EAST OF LAGUARTA, PROVINCE OF HUESCA

EMBALSE DE YESA, EAST OF PAMPLONA, PROVINCE OF NAVARRA 133

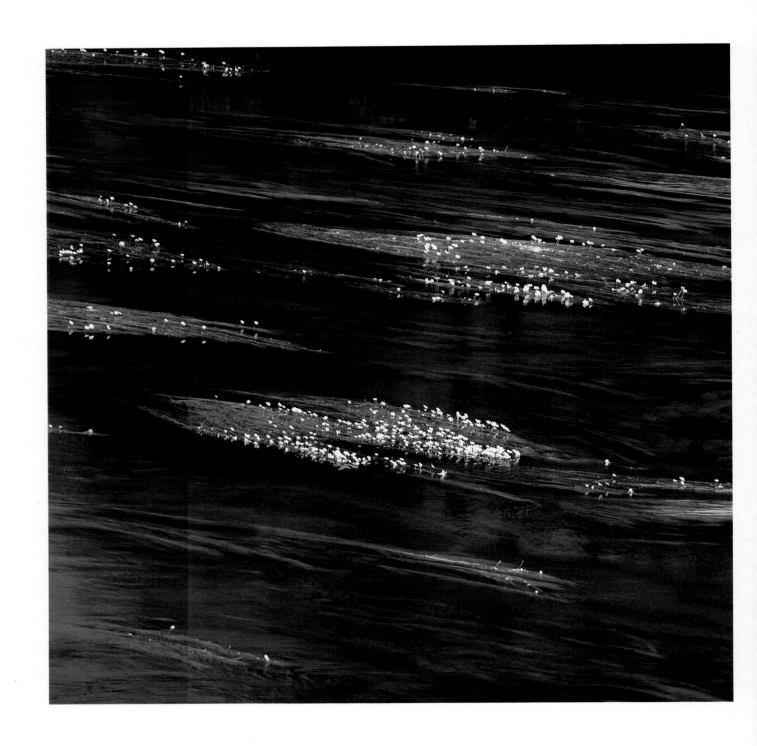

RIVER MIÑO, NORTH OF LUGO, PROVINCE OF LUGO

VALLE DE ARÁN, PROVINCE OF LÉRIDA

136   NORTH OF PINOS-PUENTE, PROVINCE OF GRANADA

SOUTH OF CHELVA, PROVINCE OF VALENCIA 137

SIERRA DE GREDOS, PROVINCE OF ÁVILA

NERJA, SOUTH OF GRANADA, PROVINCE OF GRANADA 139

EAST OF EL BURGO, PROVINCE OF MÁLAGA

WEST OF AINSA, PROVINCE OF HUESCA   141

EAST OF BAZA, PROVINCE OF GRANADA

EAST OF CÓRDOBA, PROVINCE OF CÓRDOBA